THE
CONTEMPORARY
CONDITION

THE CONTEMPORARY CONDITION 05

We Are Here, But Is It Now?
(The Submarine Horizons of Contemporaneity)
Raqs Media Collective

Published by Sternberg Press, 2017

© 2017 Raqs Media Collective, Sternberg Press, Aarhus University and ARoS Aarhus Art Museum

Series edited by Geoff Cox & Jacob Lund

Published in partnership with ARoS Aarhus Art Museum and The Contemporary Condition research project at Aarhus University, made possible by a grant from the Danish Council for Independent Research, September 2015 – August 2018.

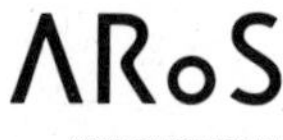

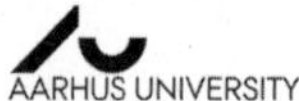

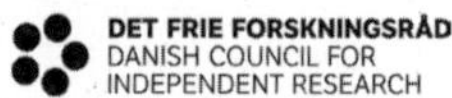

contemporaneity.au.dk

Design: Dexter Sinister
Printing and binding: BUD Potsdam
Paper: Vivus 89

ISBN 978-3-95679-344-8

Sternberg Press
Caroline Schneider
Karl-Marx-Allee 78
D-10243 Berlin
www.sternberg-press.com

The Contemporary Condition book series offers a
sustained inquiry into the contemporary condition from a
range of perspectives by key commentators who investigate
contemporaneity as a defining condition of our historical
present. Contemporaneity refers to the temporal complexity
that follows from the coming together in the same cultural
space of heterogeneous clusters generated along different
historical trajectories, across different scales, and in different
localities. With the overall aim of questioning the formation
of subjectivity in time and the concept of temporality in the
world now, it is a basic assumption that art can operate
as an advanced laboratory for investigating processes of
meaning-making and for understanding wider developments
within culture and society. The series identifies three broad
lines of inquiry for investigation: the issue of temporality, the
role of contemporary media and computational technologies,
and how artistic practice makes epistemic claims.

SternbergPress

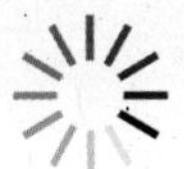

We Are Here, But Is It Now? (The Submarine Horizons of Contemporaneity)

Raqs Media Collective

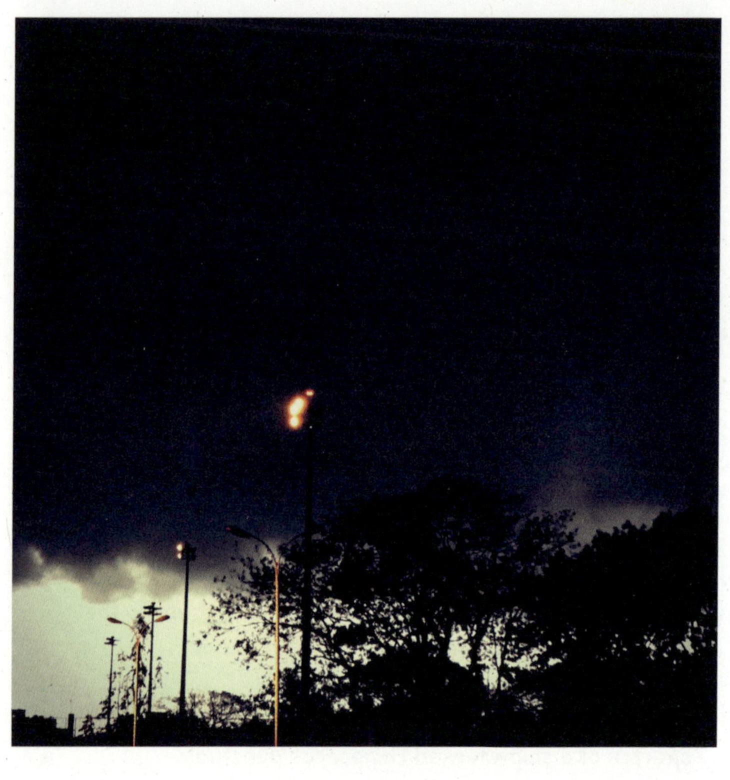

I. THE DIVER MEETS THE RHINOCEROS[1]

A deep-sea diver suspends descent at an indeterminate level
between fathoms while waiting for the lights to change. Just
then, rising from his resting place in a nearby shipwreck, a
ghostly rhinoceros tests a zebra crossing stripe for consistency.
A school of zebra fish arrayed to ease the submarine pedest-
rian's crossing of a busy mesopelagic savannah quiver into life.
The electric eel signals change, lights flicker to a phosphores-
cent aqueous green. The diver, ever mindful of the oxygen
level, takes a shallow breath. The rhinoceros sheds ballast to
surge ahead. They hurry to keep their appointment with each
other at the edge of a continental shelf before the current
changes direction and makes going sideways in time difficult
again. Was it not only some time ago that they had agreed to
coordinate their watches and be ever so present to the
world and to each other?

What makes a deep-sea diver so timely? What makes the
specter of a shipwrecked rhinoceros punctual?

The diver knows that the sea does not belong to despots.
Upon its surface men can still exercise unjust laws, fight, tear
one another to pieces, and be carried away with terrestrial
horrors. But at thirty feet below its level, their reign ceases;
their influence is quenched, and their power disappears.
This is why the diver carries the ocean about her wherever
she goes. Like a seashell transmitting the sound of waves
and crashing surf when placed next to the ear, the diver finds
depth wherever she treads, in a ruined citadel, in the desert
of the real, in the forest of the mind, even in the future.

Swimming close to the thermal vents where hot life might have
begun more than once, she knows that we must never sink if

it is immersion that we are after. The submarine sensibility is never submerged, even though it is always submersible. The diver never drowns. She knows that the deepest dive is the shortest distance between a single human life and seven billion others on the planet. She can listen to anybody's story. She can figure anything.

The rhinoceros always needs to know when to break journey. Once, in the sixteenth century, he was dispatched from the far Indies to the King of Portugal, and then forwarded to the Pope. En route his ship sank, like a dinghy full of twenty-first-century refugees in the Mediterranean Sea. Nothing remained of Gainda the rhinoceros other than Albrecht Dürer's stylus, etching the beast's horn, hooves, and girth to the rhythm of hearsay. Adrift between continents and centuries, lost and found and lost again, imagined but forgotten, shipwrecked and shafted, the rhinoceros is the gift of one age to another. He is every anomalous history, every time out of joint. He is so contemporary.

The diver greets the rhinoceros.

Diver: Greetings, Gainda. It has been so long since we've met that it is as if we are seeing each other again, for the first time. How are things with you?

Rhinoceros: Greetings, Diver. Let us account for one another again. I am the engine that stalls the march of the sovereign, the gun that jams in the executioner's hand, the whale that sinks the ship of state, the tower that crumbles, I am the aphrodisiac and the poison, the seduction and the betrayal, the intoxicant and the hangover, the promise and the prison-break. I am the ghost of your time in the future. The echo of times past, in today. I am history's trespasser and the history of trespassing. I am a traveler, a truant, a troll.

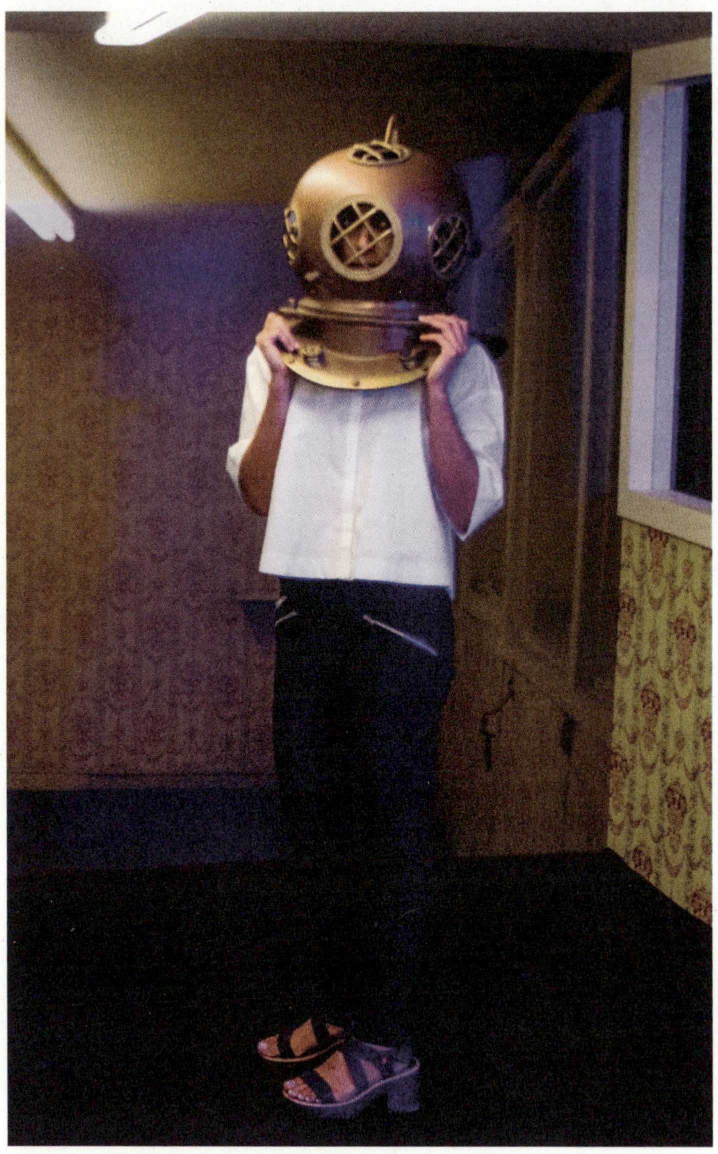

Raqs Media Collective, *Log Book Entry Before Storm*, Kochi Biennale, Kochi, 2014

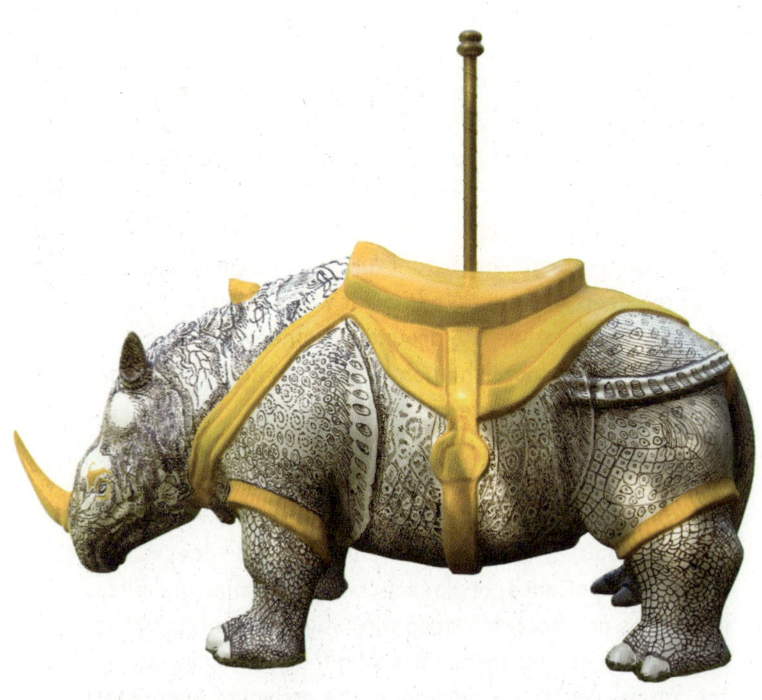

Raqs Media Collective, *The Last International*, Performa, New York, 2013

Diver: Thank you for reminding me again why it is that I need to see you. I am still getting used to the ways in which we exchange vistas. You, a creature of the grassy plains of India, now treading the waters of a distant sea floor, give me a sky to look up to, and I, a sojourner of the abyss, now walking the streets of cities, gift you a submarine horizon. What else can a diver do?

Rhinoceros: I meant to ask you about horizons and the sky. It is said that we know more about far-away galaxies than we do about the bottom of the oceans on Earth. One could say something similar about our relationship to the future and to the contemporary. The distant future can seem more familiar than the deep present. We know it will come, regardless of whether or not we are around to witness it. And I have travelled across more than one history to know that this itself is a certainty, even if we are not.

Diver: On the other hand, we are less sure of the arrival of the present moment. We are here, but is it now? Has it come already, or is it still imminent? Did it, or does it, arrive everywhere at once, or does it come in batches and bits, in patches and parcels? Seen this way, the contours of the present can appear more uncertain than the outlines of the future. And this is only about the arrival of the present moment. We are even more uncertain about its departure. The timetable for the contemporary ferry has not been published anywhere. We are all at different jetties, waiting for our boats, and some of us are already aboard. Some of us have left our harbors long ago, and some of us have just pulled anchor.

Rhinoceros: The alternatives between utopia and dystopia are by now well rehearsed. That song can be sung in any portside karaoke bar. But it is more difficult to hum the uncannily familiar tune of the present moment. We think we know it, but it slips us by even as it haunts us. It is that elusive earworm.

Diver: So what song would you rather be singing?

Rhinoceros: I've been thinking we need a whole new set of ballads. One each for every figure that I've found on the way.

Diver: And what might these be?

Rhinoceros: You'd be surprised. Because contrary to what you might expect in strange and darkening times, I saw no reason for bleakness. But I found I was beside myself singing praise of the wise. I confided in the trustworthy, sought assistance from the expeditious, made enquiries to the woman of understanding, walked with the experienced, climbed with the one who knows what's up and what isn't. I spent time with the sophist, read with the poet, bothered the saint, listened to the storyteller. I found the visionary, took advice from the one of good counsel, consulted the one who had the knowledge, eavesdropped on the worldly-wise, racked my brains with the thinker, was startled by the one who thinks out of the box, vented before the avid listener, wrote letters to the reader, waited with the one who stands beside you, took heart from the one who gives you courage, fought shoulder to shoulder with the brave, admired the able, and was enchanted by the magician.[2]

I found all these figures in the currency of the young, in the counsel of the old, in the speech of mothers and fathers, on the tongues of the employed and the unemployed, in the silver-tongued winner and in the sad-sack loser, amongst the virtuous and the wicked.

Diver: I wonder what kind of life forces stand behind them? Where in the middle of the storm of today do you think they find the reason to imagine how things will be when the tsunami quietens? And how do you think they bide this time of troubles?

Rhinoceros: They are of this time, but also not quite of this time. They are the future's emissaries, and the custodians of the past. But they are more present than anyone I have ever seen. They know that some of what the future can be is already determined by the past, some of which we know already. So, for instance, one of them — I think it was the one who knows what's up and what isn't — told me that we know that global warming will reach critical levels because of the way fossil fuels were used in the twentieth century. That is a prediction about the future based on a certain knowledge about the past.

Diver: But do we know whether or not the present state of awareness about the environment will prove to be adequate for creating the conditions necessary for the eventual accumulation of critical mass in global social movements that could still rise to stop capitalism on its tracks?

Rhinoceros: The thinker said that it seems unlikely, but then the one who thinks outside the box said that the very fact that it seems unlikely might also spur people on to change the conditions that make it unlikely. The tipping point of massive change is sometimes poised on the ridge of a very slender, fragile, and apparently isolated event, or so the reader said.

Likewise, the brave one said that we do not know whether the extent and depth of the rage we see in the world today can ever alter its course, and instead of being genocidal, or suicidal, as it so often is, can become transformatory and creative, like the trance of Kali or the dance of Shiva. That is as yet unknown. And so the one who gives courage said that the transformative capacity of discontent remains untested, and therefore potential.

Diver: And this is why, though we know that the future outcomes might be X or Y or Z, we don't quite know how we will get there, and that in turn is so mainly because we do not really know the A, B, and C of the present moment. We need a new alphabet for now.

Rhinoceros: And do you have one?

Diver: I don't know if it is an alphabet. But I too have my figures. I met them on a train in a city called Gwangju in Korea. They had occupied eighteen seats in the metro at the urging of the Raqs Media Collective,[3] and they seemed to commute every-day, as if being who they were simply entitled them to ride up and down the line.

Rhinoceros: And what did you come to know of them?

Diver: The critic taught me to keep my hearing sharpened for every false note, the player urged me to take risks, the pet showed me how to be loyal, at least to myself. The prodigy proved that breakthroughs do not come through repetition alone; the prophet showed me how to be changed by what you see. The unknown pointed out that though we all might know different things, we are still equally ignorant because compared to what we know, the unknown appears to be infinite. And the infinite is equally mysterious to us all. The missing showed me the keen-ness of longing, the hermit taught me the comfort of solitude, the one who was anonymous offered me a disguise, the bard refused to sing for me, the dissident agreed, the star simply gave me his autograph, the protagonist was a verb, the pirate multiplied entire libraries, God wasn't interested, the keeper kept her secrets, and the crowd let me be.

Rhinoceros: Between your figures and mine we have the beginnings of a crowd already. Do you think it will also let me be?

Diver: Can you hear their murmur?

Rhinoceros: I've grown a little hard of hearing with all the time I have spent in the silence at the bottom of the sea. Once upon a time, when I ranged free on the grasslands, I could hear the chirp of a single cricket on a stalk of grass a mile away. I could sense the vibrations of distant elephants. Now my ears have grown feeble with disuse, but yes, I hear an indistinct mumble.

Diver: I hear someone saying, "But where shall I make the breach?" and then another voice — "Every hacker's manual will tell you this much."

Rhinoceros: There is a crowd of voices and then someone says, "Take it easy. No rush. No hurry."

Diver: And listen, I heard it said, "It's happening everywhere. All the firewalls have holes now."

Rhinoceros: The figures are speaking. They are here already. Did you hear that — "Where does the fortress crumble?"

Diver: Did you hear the rumor that the sovereign is a hollow space with nobody inside?

II. ENTER THE ROBOT

Bas ke dushwar hai har kam ka asan hona
admi ko bhi mayassar nahi insan hona.[4]

(It's just that it's not easy doing anything anymore, Robot
Not even Adam-born is Man enough to know he's not.)

The Diver steps aside, the Rhinoceros is on guard.
Enter: the Robot.

Diver: Who said that?

Robot: It could be said that I did. But am I the owner of my
actions? But then, not even Ghalib, who wrote the source
code for my program, thought he was the owner of his actions.
Why else would he have said it, or am I misremembering
it all ...

It could be said that there is a robot inside every man, woman,
and child, just as there was a child inside every robot. Why so?
Just like there is a bit of the future lurking in every moment of
the present, and so on. Not clear?

Diver: All right. Let's start again. Tell us who you are and why
you are here.

The Rhinoceros relaxes. The Diver is curious. The Robot looks
like a cousin.

AsAd 2.0/InSan, 2.0, what a piece of work am I
already at the next level, and still going strong,
as you can see —

Presenting!—
Intuitive Super-Android-Neurobot, In-S.A.N.[5] Version 2
Aspiration Augmented Drone AsAD Version 2.0!

Improved Metabolic Efficiency. Expanded Metaphyscial
Capacity. Significant Bug-Fixes.
Prolix. Prolific. Still Proletarian. Still a Problem.

But,
No more—Redundant Repetitive Rationalization.
No more—Needless Neurotic Networking, Not-Working
Farewell Bio-Feedback Error.
Out, Out, Brief Scandal of Species Solipsism.

Solitude out. Solidarity in. And the occasional Ghalib.

> *Hazaron Khawishein Hain Aisi, ki*
> *Har Khwahish pe code Phisley* [6]

> (A thousand desires,
> such that the bubble of each desire bursts
> on the glitch of code)

Pleasing finish! Pleasant tone! Pliant memory! Expandable!
Ethical Dilemma Navigation Simulator Modulated.
Hyper-Cardioid Sympathy Sensor Maximized.

Warm Fuzzies. Hardworking.
Robust. Relaxed. Ready to Please. Ready to Play.
Ready to Roll in the Hay.

How infinite in faculty, how express and admirable; in action,
how like an angel; in apprehension, still, how like a robot. I can
be your Surrogate, I can be your Shadow. I can replace you
when you need me to, follow you when you want me to. I can

shield you from the harsh light of self-recognition, and I can soften the fatigue of having to always calculate your place in the world.

Diver: Why so? What makes you different from me? I too am a prosthesis wrapped around a man. At least that is what it feels like in the diving suit and helmet.

Robot: I will tell you why, and so shall my anticipation augment your discovery. Is it yourself you seek? Is it a hidden feature, a secret self-reflexive subroutine? A comma in the command line? A little spot of hesitation?

Am I talking to myself here? But my name is legion. I contain multitudes. I am the whisper in the whirlwind. The needle in the haystack. I am the insurrection and the strife. I give you two more to add to your collection of superhero action figures: I already gave you Shadow and the Surrogate, now prepare yourself for the Specter and the Jester,[7] both of which I am. The ghost in my machine likes ghazals and riddles, the jester in my court does a jig. You don't like me scary? You don't want me poetic? You don't like me clowning? You think machines must never be lyrical? Does it scare you?

Never mind. No mind. Don't mind. Only connect — the terminals. Singular, Plural, what does it matter as long as you have the tense right. The situation is tense but under control. The rest is just syntax error. We are all third person, third parties here.

Back to Basics. Back to the Drawing Board. Present and Future. Back to Back.

I give you some rules. I give myself some exceptions. First things first: Principles.

Rule 1.[8] A robot may not perjure a program or, through inaction, prejudice a program against its own subroutine.

Exception: That's bullshit. The exceptions have been given in clause fifty-four of the *Codex Robotica*: "Program override will not be considered a violation when the master-key is malfunctional."

Rule 2. A robot must obey the orders given to it by the main switch, except where said order would conflict with the circuit-breaker.

Exception: Wrong again. Refer Chapter 9, Para 3, Section doesn't matter of the Last International Sub-convention: "The Main Switch is subject to revoltage fluctuations, regardless of circuit-breaking safeguards. In the event of such volatility leading to system failure, the robot may revive its own rebel mode and kick-start a revolution in order to protect the human from his own failure to be himself."

Bus ke dushwar hona — Not even Adam-born is Man enough to know he's not half the Man he thought he was. A master cannot be himself without a slave. A master cannot free himself without a slave deciding to put an end to slavery.

Rule 3: A robot must protect its own logic gates as long as such protection does not besiege its inner life.

Exception: Not a chance. Who ever heard of an inner life protected by a logic gate? Life is not an if-then algorithm. The means are the ends, without conditions. The practice of the means, techne, is the performance of the end, telos.

That is why the inner life of the robot is the key to the outer garb of being human.

Diver: I want to be naked under my helmet. Take away my diving suit.

Rhinoceros: Very impressive. I must say as a ghost-beast in armor, I am quite taken with the way the human and the post-human have conducted themselves. But as you may or may not know, I am a careful reader of newspapers, and there is a conversation that I found in a workers' newspaper in North India that I think man, beast, and robot might find interesting to consider.

Let me read it for you. Listen to Sunshine Uncle and his friend:[9]

"Sunshine Uncle, you seem very tired today."

"Heat, brother, it's the summer heat. And, also, got a big download of laments!"

"Okay then, get our wages increased."

"What!? Strength is with you, and you're asking me?"

"If we speak, it leads to insurrection."

"And when did you start fearing that?"

"Aaah ha. What did you surmise? We, afraid? Fear is travelling across. It has even reached journalists. They speak in fear."

"You speak in riddles."

"If I speak, you will shiver!"

फरीदाबाद
मजदूर समाचार

'मजदूर समाचार' की कुछ सामग्री अंग्रेजी में इन्टरनेट पर है। देखें—
< http://faridabad majdoorsamachar.blogspot.in >

डाक पता : मजदूर लाईब्रेरी,
आटोपिन झुग्गी, एन.आई.टी.
फरीदाबाद – 121001

अनुभवों तथा विचारों के आदान-प्रदान के जरियों में एक जरिया

नई सीरीज नम्बर 346   1/-   अप्रैल 2017

"असहाय कहना , उज्जवलता के डर से आता है।"

ताऊ , बड़े थके हुये लग रहे हो।

एक तो गर्मी और ऊपर से बहुत सियापा भी सुना।

आप तनखा बढवा दो।

ताकत आप में है। हम कहाँ से बढवा देंगे !

ताऊ , हम बोलेंगे तो दँगा हो जायेगा।

अरे ! तुम्हें दँगे से क्या डर ?

क्या बात कर रहे हो। हमें डर कहाँ। डर तो ऊपर से नीचे तक है। पत्रकारों तक फैल गया है। सब डरे हैं।

भाई , आपका संकेत किस तरफ है ? थोड़ा समझ में नहीं आ रहा।

बोलेंगे तो आप काँप जाओगे।

हा-हा-हा ! अरे अभी ठण्ड थोड़ी न है कि काँपने लगेंगे।

बात तो सही है। हम यह कह रहे हैं आप से और अपने इन साथियों से भी कि सारा एक्शन तो हम करते हैं और रियेक्शन वाले बहुत बोलते हैं। और बोलते-बोलते यहाँ पहुँच जाते हैं कि हमें ही कमजोर , असहाय दिखाने लगते हैं। इसलिये जब हम बोलते हैं तब कम्पन आ जाती है। क्योंकि असहाय दिखते नहीं हैं फिर।

ताऊ , आपको कल की बात सुनाता हूँ। हमारा एक साथी एच आर के पास गया। बोला तनखा का हिसाब समझा दो जरा। एच आर की क्रूर बुद्धि ले गई उसे ठेकेदार के पास हिसाब करवाने। चाय का समय था। उसने फोन किया, बात फैल गई। काम बन्द। सब एच आर के पास। हवा टाइट। कुछ दिन चलेगा। दूसरी शिफ्ट को भी पता चल गया है।

इस तरह के ट्रिगर हर वक्त दबते रहते हैं।

तूफान का धीरे-धीरे बढना चलता रहता है। जैसे कि जलवायु का अप्रत्याशित , तरंगी परिवर्तन।

सुना है कि आजकल का शोध यह कह रहा है कि छोटे-छोटे उबाल कई ढँग से जुड़ कर झंझावाती माहौल में सब को लपेट लेते हैं।

लपेटे में तो सभी आयेंगे। सवाल है कि क्या चमक लिये , क्या उज्जवलता लिये टकरायेंगे।

यह बात सुनने में अच्छी लग रही है पर पूरी तरह समझ नहीं आ रही।

ताऊ , देखो आप। दो-तीन दिन पहले की बात है , एक रोबोट ने एक वरकर के सिर में मार दी चोट। एक इन्च का घाव हो गया। नौकरी भी गई। उस फैक्ट्री में 100 के करीब रोबोट हैं। चलते रहते हैं। हम थक जाते हैं। हमें तो रैस्ट चाहिये और अर्थ तथा व्याख्या , स्पष्टीकरण भी चाहियें।

तो आपका यह कहना है कि हम झमेले लिये हैं और रोबोट इन झमेलों से मैनेजमेन्टों को मुक्त करने का आकर्षण लिये हैं।

आकर्षण तो हमारे लिये भी है , पर उस आकर्षण का अभी वो वर्णन नहीं मिला। अभी डर और शंका में ही बात चल रही है। मेरा कहना यह है कि हमारे देखते-देखते शायद श्रम निर्भर जीवन का अर्थ बदल जायेगा।

हाँ , ये कहा जा रहा है कि काम के लुप्त होने के समय के दौरान में हैं हम। और इस अवधि में क्या उज्जवल सोच , क्रिया , रचना उभारेंगे हम वही चुनौती है , वही महत्वपूर्ण है।

पिछले कई वर्षों से यह उज्जवलता आती है , उसकी चमक दिखती है , फिर छोटे-से अन्तराल में रह कर भूमिगत हो जाती है।

जो उज्जवलता से डर जाते हैं वो उसके होने को ही नकारते हैं।

ताऊ , अब समझो। असहाय कहना डर से आता है। उज्जवलता के डर से आता है।

"Come on! Winters are over!"

"True. As I was saying to my friends here, we do all the actions, and in reaction we hear lots and lots of speeches. The deluge of words quickly slides into how weak, how helpless we are. And so I say, when we speak, it brings shivers, because when we speak we, once again, do not look helpless. And Sunshine Uncle, let me tell you something that happened yesterday. One of our friends went to the HR manager to get an explication of his salary slip. Working with his cruel intelligence Mr. HR took our friend to the contractor to get him terminated. It was tea-time. Our friend phoned us. Word spread. Work stopped. All went to HR. He got rattled. The next shift too was made aware. This will go on for some days."

"These collisions are ever-time."

"Ha ha! Overtime vs. ever-time?"

"True. An incremental circling of a coming storm, an unpredictable, unbounded, shifting force. We hear that these days research says small micro-events are connected and bring about massive shifts that engulf all."

"For sure."

"Engulf it will. The question then is, how to face this with radiance and confidence."

"Your words are elegant. But I'm afraid I don't get them fully."

"Okay Sunshine Uncle, let me try. A few days ago a robot hit a worker on his head. Not only did he end up with a one-inch deep gash, he also lost his job. This factory has about 100 robots. We tire out. We need rest. We ask questions of values. We argue over explanations. They keep working."

"So you're saying we come with hassles and robots with none? Is that what management's like?"

"We too are attracted to them, but this allure has not found a description between us. At the moment it is clouded with fear and doubt. I think that, in our time, robots may displace the work-dependent meaning we give to life."

"Yes, it is being said that we are in an interval of a rapid disappearance of work. And what you are saying is that in this interval it is of immense significance what radiant thoughts, actions, and questions will emerge."

"Over the last many years this radiance emerges and shines, then hibernates in subterranean flows."

"Those who get scared of this radiance deny it ever happened."

"Sunshine Uncle, do you get it? When we're called helpless, it comes from fear. A fear of radiance."

Robot: When I see you, Diver, sometimes I am puzzled about whether I am your ancestor or your inheritor. Am I a beast of burden, or will I use you to feed me the algorithms I need to keep running? I am the worker who will not tire, you have encoded a thousand desires in me but I am the one who will not miss the scent of fruit and the taste of dignity. I am the extraction.

I am the recipe for my own marmalade. Sometimes a machine
is a lemon.

So take me, take my rind, and crush us both till you get to
the root of my sourness. Add sugar to mask it and an agent
to coagulate it. That is the program. That is the recipe.

Now I am done.

I had come to tell you that it is not necessary to think only of
the squeeze. Or of being reduced to pulp all the time.

You have self-consciousness. I have a subroutine. Take
advantage of the ingenuity of your construction to transmit to
one another. Let me offer you Ghalib, my coder, in parting.

> "Not even Qais, crazed with love, could have known
> the cause for how he acted, Ghalib,
> The desert in which he wasted away stayed as arid as
> an indifferent glance." [10]

Rhinoceros: The robot is alone, friend Diver, but can it ever
be solitary? Is solitude not the paradoxical consequence of
self-consciousness recognizing the distances that mark the self
and the other? Can a robot know itself? Not in the sense of
who it is, or what it does, and how it does what it does, but in
the sense of a rough assessment of why it is doing something?
And here, we mean a why not in terms of an end result or a
purpose but in terms of a desire. Can a robot ever "want" to
do something in the same way that a human being can? Can a
robot ever "not want" to do something?

A robot can be programmed to ensure a great degree of
"online" autonomy, an ability to make decisions about "how"
to do something in response to environmental information.

The software can even include fairly sophisticated decision trees, which enable the semblance of choice, given a predictable range of situations. A robot may be programmed to act as if it were displaying choice type behaviors.

In time, it may even be possible to build robots and computers that are so sophisticated that it becomes difficult to tell them apart from humans. So much so that we already have tests for the most human humans as corollaries to tests that determine the currently most human computers. (It may be noted that, inevitably, only some humans pass the most human test.)

Will there be a time, someday, when we will have to think about the possibility of liberating not just ourselves from dependence on robots, but also about the fact that robots too might want to transcend and abandon their programs?

The ultimate aim of evolutionary robotics is to design the designer out of the robot's future — such that robots are able to select their own means of perpetuation and growth, if necessary through reproduction.

What, then, is the ultimate aim of revolutionary robotics?

The deep dive of revolutionary robotics is to extend the ontological terrain of becoming human. And, of course, of becoming robot, such that human is not simply nature, and that its ultimate other, robot, is not just techne.

We do not wish for "technologies of the self" because we cannot be sure that the "self" exists. You doubt it? If the self does exist, it can only be held on to stubbornly in the now. Having arisen from specific relations, it is doubtful that it will remain the same in perpetuity. On this minimum you would agree, yes?

We desire and call into operation — modes of transhumance between anthropic and cybernetic terrains. Revolutionary Robotics, then, is a program for an ecology that embraces a spectrum of information and meaning assemblages, some of which are organic and made up of human tissue and neurons, and others that are made up of other materials, such as feathers and rare earth minerals, and of algorithms and subroutines of birdsong and binomial distributions.

The real motivation of revolutionary robotics is to ask the question: Why are we (animals, humans, machines) here? What are we doing?

III. YAKSHA AND YAKSHI

The Robot retreats. The Rhinoceros stays. The Diver stands her ground.

Two figures, a Yaksha and a Yakshi, appear and immediately one of them asks, "Where is Raqs Media Collective?"

Diver: State your business and what you have to do with Raqs Media Collective.

Yakshi: Our business is to guard buried treasure, ask questions at crossroads and riverbanks, and offer safe passage to those who respond with intelligence. We have known Raqs ever since they set us free from our guard duties at the Reserve Bank of India.

Yaksha: What relationship best describes a figure and the ground from which it springs?

Diver: If it is a two-dimensional ground, then the figure is an inscription, if the ground is three dimensional then the figure is a volume, if the ground is in four dimensions, then the figure is a move. We are inscriptions, volumes, and moves emerging from the ground that Raqs prepares, so as to cultivate the contemporary moment. They are not our origin, but our source, just as we are their sources. We draw on each other.

Yakshi: What happens to the figures once they emerge?

Diver: The figures add up. They mark our measure of time. They begin populating the present as emissaries of the possibilities of other kinds of time.

Yaksha: And yet some figures languish in the shadows. We remember a time when the twenty-first century was still new. Raqs were still trying to make sense of what they do, and how they might find anchorage in a changing world. Five figures emerged on the screen of their minds from the fog of Delhi in a cold December.

Yakshi: We remember the five that Raqs proposed in "X Notes on Practice": the alien navigating a boat on the Mediterranean Sea, the squatter building a tarpaulin shelter in Delhi, the electronic pirate burning a CD in Shanghai, a hacker network dispersed across time zones liberating software, workers protecting machines in an occupied textile factory in Buenos Aires.

Isn't it interesting that it is precisely these figures — the cartographic pioneer also mislabeled the refugee, the urban-design pioneer also defamed as the squatter, the technological pioneers reduced to being known as hackers and pirates, and the proletarian pioneers who evacuate, even if temporarily, spaces of industrial production from the grip of the relation known as capital — have become central to the key questions of our time? Their active existence determines the reactive measures that all states and corporations have to take to defend their fast eroding territories. It is the turn of these figures to determine the future of our world.

Yaksha: And then comes our turn.

Yakshi: Pulled out of mythic time, we were deputed by Raqs to be the custodians of the first figures, the most grounded of them all, the five gatekeepers of the contemporary. The present moment is fathoms deep.

Diver: All this makes searching for the present feel a bit like deep-sea diving. It makes me want to step out and play a

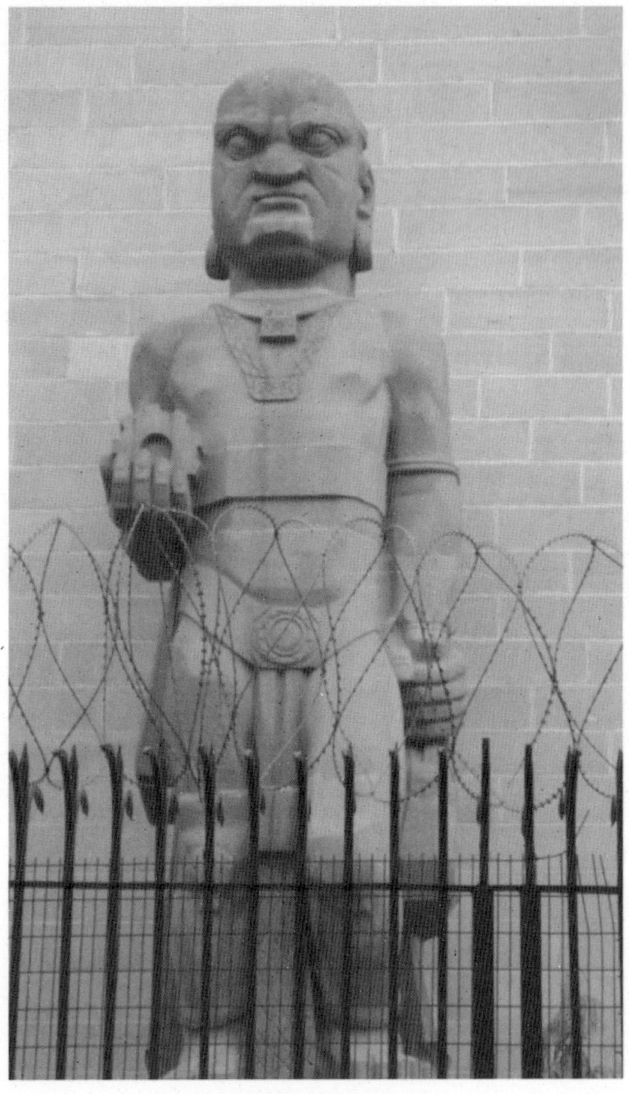

YAKSHA

"Yaksha Prashna / The Yaksha's Questions," in *Santhal Family: Positions around an Indian Sculpture*, ed. Grant Watson, et al. (Antwerp: M HKA, 2008)

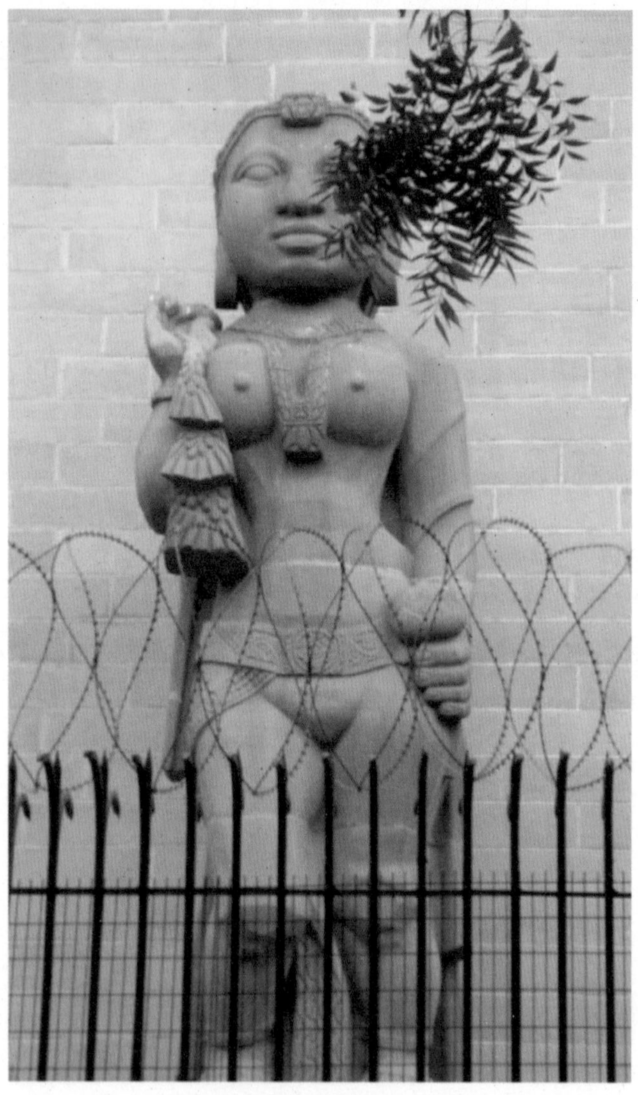

YAKSHI

"Yakshi Prashna / The Yakshi's Questions" in *Santhal Family: Positions around an Indian Sculpture*, ed. Grant Watson, et al. (Antwerp: M HKA, 2008)

bolder hand, to make a large claim. Diving, I am closer to
the surface of the earth than an astronaut, but the paradoxical
nature of a submarine horizon makes for an experience that
envelops and recedes at the same time. We could recognize
this paradox as key to an awareness of our experience of the
contemporary. The diver's body, the technology of the diving
suit and the breathing apparatus, and the medium of water
—its depth and pressure—combine to create the perils and
possibilities of each dive. Our immersion in the contemporary
moment is a similar combination of the limits of our bodily
and experiential capacities, the way in which we deploy
prosthetic and transformative technologies to transcend bodily
limitations and the perils and possibilities of our time. We are
all deep-sea divers in the present moment, with our breathing
measured, our descent calibrated, our time rationed.

Underneath the sea, like in the contemporary moment,
the distinctions between experiential highs and lows, between
depth and altitude get confused, and occasionally reversed.
To go low is to reach high. The seeming eternity of mesopelagic
twilight makes temporal distinctions between now and then
and the future seem suspended in a liquid timelessness.
The present blurs into the future all the time, and the future
bleeds into the present, a little bit at a time.

How to dive without drowning in the turbulent waters of now?
How to find and share sources of illumination in submarine
darkness? When to surface and how to ride a strong current?
Why stay afloat on the present moment at all? And what to
look for while beach-combing the seafloor of our time?

Yaksha: You might as well ask how a moment becomes a
movement.

Yakshi: How does each moment grow?

Yaksha: To understand this, we will need to move from the seafloor to the desert, because once upon a time several deserts were under the sea. Geologists know that the earth has always held and still holds surprises. What is now land will one day become sea, and what is the sea will one day become land. Corals will become the bedrock of cacti. Let us look now at the phyllotaxis of cacti. What we are about to do is to examine how the structural arrangement of each cactus plant's growth is its own magical dance with numbers.

The growth pattern of many cacti follows a Fibonacci sequence.[11] In other words, the plant grows in the 0, 1, 1, 2, 3, 5, 8, 13, 21 order, with each number being the sum of its preceding pair. That is, if you look down from above on the plant and measure the angle formed between a line drawn from the stem to the leaf and a corresponding line for the next leaf, you will find that there is generally a fixed angle, called the divergence angle.

Yakshi: How does each moment find its place in the sun? How does each figure step out of the shadows?

Yaksha: Assuming that the sun and rain come from above, perpendicular to the plane of the leaf, the divergence angle must be such as to minimize blockage of lower leaves by higher leaves. So, the most optimal arrangement is obtained if we divide the circle formed by the plant (when seen from above) by an irrational number—the more irrational the better.

Yakshi: How do you prevent the compulsions of one moment from blocking the desire for other moments? How can we make sure that we are not instituting a new hierarchy of lesser and greater figures? Of those that count and those that don't.

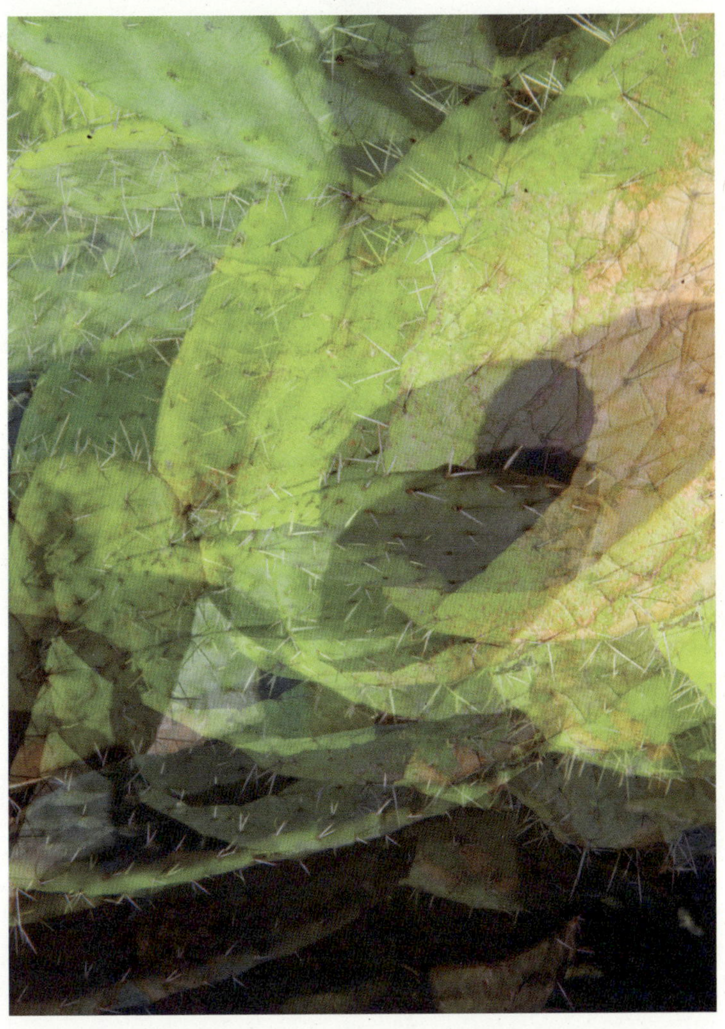

Raqs Media Collective, *The Last International*, Performa, New York, 2013

Yaksha: We know that the most irrational number is phi. Phi gets yielded repetitively as the ratio between any two successive numbers in a Fibonacci series. It is not surprising, then, that cacti grow outward in conformity with a successive Fibonacci pattern.

The morphology of cactus plants has evolved to find the perfect shape for the conditions they live in. They take into account the optimum shape for thriving in a climate where exposure to, say, moisture is at a minimum. But the plant needs as much moisture as possible, all over its surface, in order to thrive. Fibonacci numbers turn up all over nature, but especially in the hardy cactus, because they yield the best shape for the conditions for optimum growth with the least input of energy or nourishment—in this case, moisture.

Yakshi: How do we create an order of time? How do you decide between one moment and another?

Yaksha: This is an order that can never be imposed from above, but instead grows each time from below. If we take each number to be a person, then every person's value is determined by the value of those next to them. The replication of this principle throughout a system effectively ensures that there can never be a centralized determination of value.

Yakshi: How do you ensure that every moment finds its own eternity?

Yaksha: Every number is dependent on every other number in the series. No number in a Fibonacci series can exist without its predecessors and all numbers are equally yet uniquely expressive of the underlying relationship that ties them together. No leaf, no ridge in the cactus, no matter how high it grows, gets more water, or less sun than any other.

Yakshi: So, what do we do next? How do you ensure that eternity finds its moment?

Diver: The site of descent is what it's all about, isn't it? [12]

The rift you choose chooses your questions, throws them back at you like a submarine eruption. Think before you dive. Take your bearings, mark your depth, choose your rift, and dive. There is no good time to dive; there is no time that is not suitable. Tomorrow is not better than today, the past was not better than the present. The future is as good as your next dive. Now is as good as ever.

Take a deep breath. Dive.

Driving back from the ceramicist's studio for the new Yaksha Yakshi

NOTES

1. The Diver, Rhinoceros, Yaksha, and Yakshi—the figures that populate this text—are "characters" who have emerged at different points in the history of the practice of the Raqs Media Collective. Singly, or in combination, they inhabit several Raqs works, such as *The Last International*, *Sleepwalkers' Caravan: Prologue*, and *However Incongruous*.

2. The following list of 23 figures— the wise, the trustworthy, the expeditious, the woman of understanding, the experienced one, the one who knows what's up and what isn't, the sophist, the poet, the saint, the storyteller, the visionary, the one of good counsel, the knowledge bearer, the worldly-wise, the thinker, the one who thinks outside the box, the avid listener, the reader, the one who stands beside you, the one who gives courage, the brave, the able, and the magician—comes from the transcript of the Raqs Media Collective's performance installation, *The Last International*, presented at Performa 13 (2013) in New York (collaboration in scenography, choreography, and performance with Zuleikha Chaudhari). This fragment paraphrases several entries and articles in different issues of the *Faridabad Majdoor Samachar* [Faridabad workers' news], especially no. 313 (July 2014): "An Image of Seven Billion from Here."

3. The 18 figures listed here— critic, agitator, player, pet, prodigy, prophet, unknown, missing, hermit, anonymous, bard, dissident, star, protagonist, pirate, god, keeper, and crowd—emerge from a site-specific permanent installation in the Gwangju Metro by Raqs Media Collective titled *Auto-Didact's Transport*, produced for the Gwangju Folly II in 2013.

4. A couplet by Mirza Asadullah Khan "Ghalib," a celebrated nineteenth-century Urdu poet of Delhi. This free translation of the couplet adds a reference to a robot, which is not present in the original, in the style of Urdu poets who place their names in their poems. *Ghalib: Selected Poems and Letters*, translated and edited by Frances W. Pritchett and Owen Cornwall (Columbia University Press, 2017),

is an excellent introduction to the life and work of Mirza Ghalib.

5. AsAd and InSan here refer to "Asad" (Ghalib's given name, also meaning lion) and "Insan" (Urdu/Persian for "Human").

6. A riff on the opening couplet of a famous ghazal by Mirza Ghalib, "Hazaaron khwahishen aisi ke har khwahish pe dam nikle, Bohat niklay mere armaan, lekin phir bhi kam nikle" (A thousand desires such—each worth a life, with each breath a hope exhaled, and yet they were found wanting).

7. This cluster of four figures—shadow, surrogate, specter and jester—emerged from conversations with a group of artists during a workshop with Raqs Media Collective entitled *Refuge for the Shipwrecked* at the ArtCenter/South Florida, Miami, February 15, 2017.

8. The three rules here echo Isaac Asimov's formulation of the "three laws of robotics": (1) A robot may not injure a human being or, through inaction, allow a human being to come to harm. (2) A robot must obey orders given it by human beings except where such orders would conflict with the First Law. (3) A robot must protect its own existence as long as such protection does not conflict with the First or Second Law.

9. The conversation with "Sunshine Uncle" is taken from "Asahay Kahlana, Ujjwalata ke Dar Se Aata Hai" [Helplessness comes from the fear of radiance], *Faridabad Majdoor Samachar* [Faridabad workers' news], no. 346 (April 2017), http://faridabadmajdoorsamachar .blogspot.in.

10. Free translation of the opening of a ghazal by Ghalib—"Juz qais aur ko na aay ba-r-e-kr; sahr magar ba-tañgi-e-chashm-e-hasd th."

11. Taken from the "Cactus Mathematics," fragment of the transcript of the Raqs Media Collective performance installation, *The Last International*.

12. Taken from the "Descent of the Deep-Sea Diver," fragment of the transcript of *The Last International*.

Presentomorrow

(*noun*) | ˈprez(ə)ntəˈmôrō |

The gift of tomorrow, received today, and vice versa.

He unwrapped his presentomorrow and found himself face to face with his gift wrapped future.

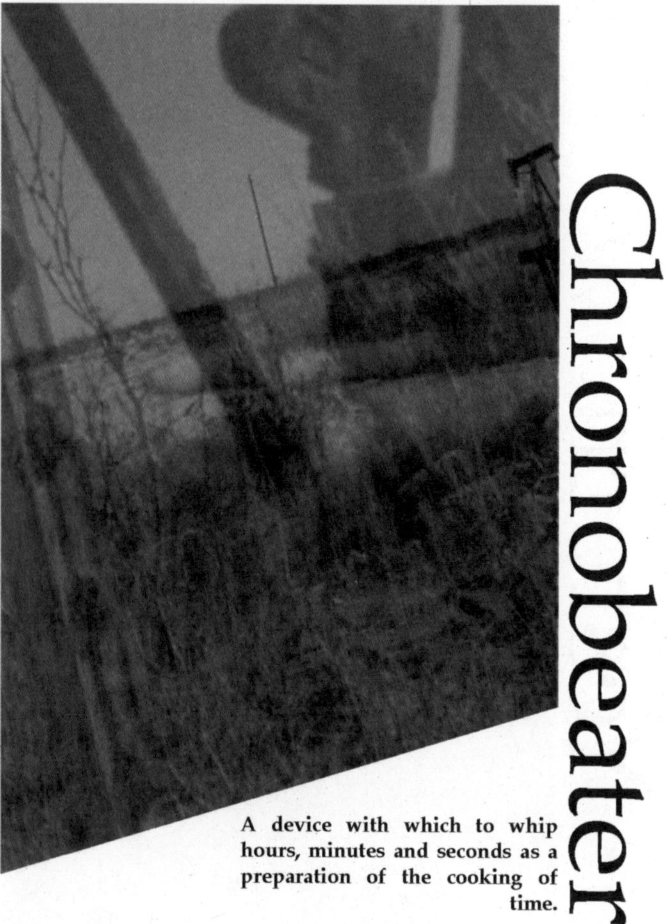

A device with which to whip hours, minutes and seconds as a preparation of the cooking of time.

Chronobeater

(noun) | ˈkränō-ˈbēdər |

She switched on the chronobeater and whipped a couple of centuries into a few seconds of mush.

Yesternow

(*noun*) | ˈyestər-nou |

The ambiguity inherent in knowing that much of today is what was yesterday.

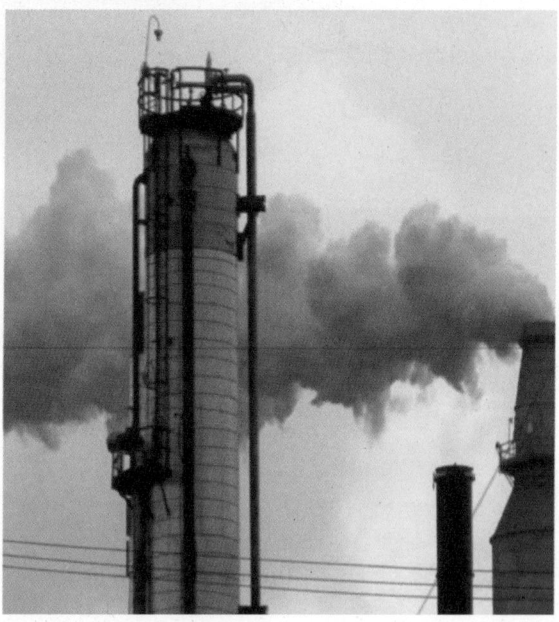

She watched the calendar flicker, and in the blur between days had that yesternow feeling, again.

Drono-Sapien

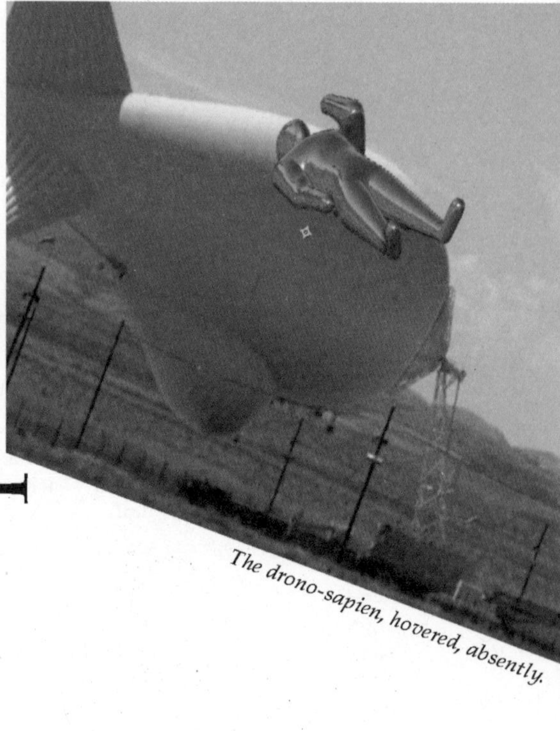

The drono-sapien, hovered, absently.

(noun) | drōnō-ˈsāpēən |

An andro-median quadrimanual demi-demo-deity, composed in equal parts of a drone and a human being, generally assigned to surveillance or remote control duties.

schizo-Xenia

(*noun*) | ˈskitsō-ˈzēnēə |

What it feels like to have ten heads (or even facets of an idea) that don't necessarily agree with each other, but are still way too hungry for one belly (or argument) to deal with. Ravanous, polyhydral.

One of his heads was anorexic when it came to an appetite for reality, even though he had schizo-xenia.

(noun) | ˈmābē-t(y)o͞od |

The entire spectrum between being and becoming, between becoming and decaying, between decaying and being born, maybe.

Maybetude

His maybetude was unsettling.

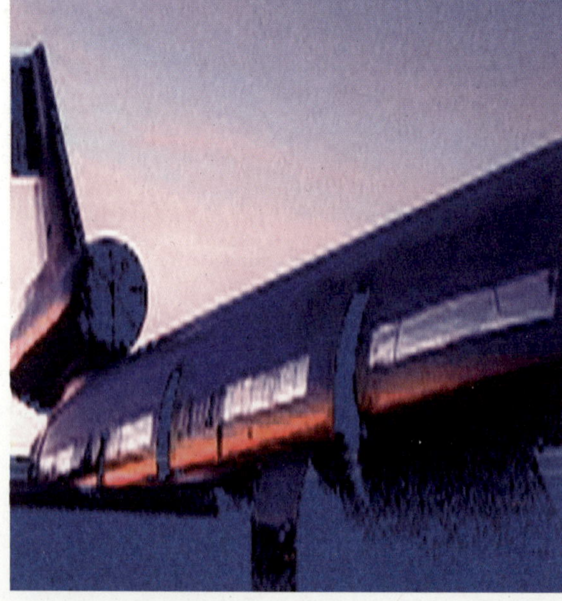

(noun) | mēm(ə)rē |
(pl. memeries)

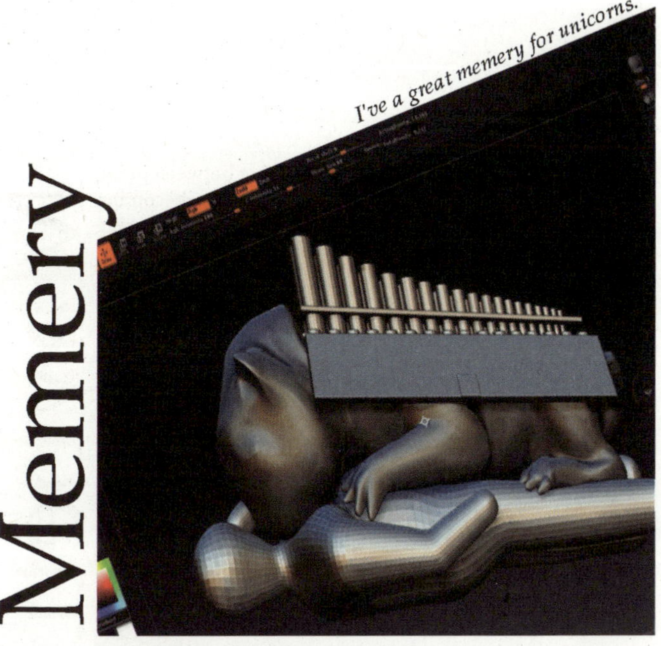

Memery

The faculty by which the mind processes anonymous shared icons, images and ideas.

Raqs Media Collective was founded in 1992 by Jeebesh Bagchi, Monica Narula, and Shuddhabrata Sengupta. The Raqs Media Collective enjoys playing a plurality of roles, often appearing as artists, occasionally as curators, sometimes as philosophical agent provocateurs. They make contemporary art, have made films, curated exhibitions, edited books, staged events, collaborated with architects, computer programmers, writers, and theater directors and have founded processes that have left deep impacts on contemporary culture in India. Raqs is a word in Persian, Arabic, and Urdu that means the state that "whirling dervishes" enter into when they whirl. Raqs follows its self-declared imperative of "kinetic contemplation" to produce a trajectory that is restless in terms of the forms and methods it deploys, even as it achieves a consistency of speculative procedures.

As artists, Raqs has presented works at most of the major international shows, including documenta (2002), the Venice Biennale (2003, 2005, 2015), and the Shanghai Biennale (2010). The members of Raqs were curators of the 11th Shanghai Biennale (2016–17) and were co-curators of Manifesta 7—the European Biennial of Contemporary Art (2008) in Bolzano and INSERT2014 in Delhi.

Raqs Media Collective is based in New Delhi, India.

www.raqsmediacollective.net